EXPLORING ENERGY TECHNOLOGY

GEOTHERMAL ENERGY

EDITED BY ELIZABETH LACHNER

Britannica Educational Publishing
IN ASSOCIATION WITH
ROSEN
EDUCATIONAL SERVICES

Published in 2019 by Britannica Educational Publishing (a trademark of Encyclopædia Britannica, Inc.) in association with The Rosen Publishing Group, Inc.
29 East 21st Street, New York, NY 10010.

Distributed exclusively by Rosen Publishing.
To see additional Britannica Educational Publishing titles, go to rosenpublishing.com.

First Edition

Britannica Educational Publishing
J.E. Luebering: Executive Director, Core Editorial
Andrea R. Field: Managing Editor, Compton's by Britannica

Rosen Publishing
Amelie von Zumbusch: Editor
Brian Garvey: Series Designer/Book Layout
Cindy Reiman: Photography Manager
Nicole DiMella: Photo Researcher

Library of Congress Cataloging-in-Publication Data

Names: Lachner, Elizabeth, editor.
Title: Geothermal energy / edited by Elizabeth Lachner.
Description: New York : Britannica Educational Publishing, in Association with Rosen Educational Services, 2019 | Series: Exploring energy technology | Audience: Grades 5–8. | Includes bibliographical references and index.
Identifiers: LCCN 2018014133| ISBN 9781508106166 (library bound) |
ISBN 9781508106159 (pbk.)
Subjects: LCSH: Geothermal resources—Juvenile literature. | Geothermal power plants—Juvenile literature.
Classification: LCC GB1199.5 .G45275 2018 | DDC 333.8/8—dc23
LC record available at https://lccn.loc.gov/2018014133

Manufactured in the United States of America

Photo credits: Cover 4FR/E+/Getty Images; cover, back cover and interior pages (background) © iStockphoto.com/tolokonov; pp. 4-5 © Gretar Ívarsson; pp. 6, 9, 11, 12, 16, 21, 24, 25 © Encyclopædia Britannica, Inc.; p. 15 © Stockbyte/Thinkstock; p. 19 Mirek Nowaczyk/Shutterstock.com; p. 28 Robert Hoetink/Shutterstock.com; p. 30 Boyloso/Shutterstock.com; p. 32 Pi-Lens/Shutterstock.com; p. 35 MakDill/Shutterstock.com; p. 38 © AP Images; p. 39 Alexander Piragis/Shutterstock.com; p. 40 Bloomberg/Getty Images.

CONTENTS

INTRODUCTION

Geothermal energy is heat that comes from inside Earth. It can be used for cooking, bathing, and heating. It can also be converted into electricity. Geothermal energy from natural pools and hot springs has been used throughout history, including by Native Americans and the ancient Greeks and Romans.

Geothermal energy is available anywhere on Earth's surface. In some places, such as Iceland, the heat is so close to the surface it can be easily used as an energy source. In Iceland, most homes are heated by hot water tapped from volcanic springs. Greenhouses heated in the same way provide fresh vegetables and fruits to this subarctic island. In other places holes must be drilled down through rocks to reach the heat.

The amount of usable energy from geothermal sources varies considerably. Geothermal energy is best found in areas with high thermal

This is the Nesjavellir Geothermal Power Plant, in Iceland. It is used to generate electricity and to supply hot water, which is used both for bathing and for heating.

gradients. Those gradients occur in regions affected by recent volcanic activity, in areas located along plate boundaries (such as along the Pacific Ring of Fire), or in areas marked by thin

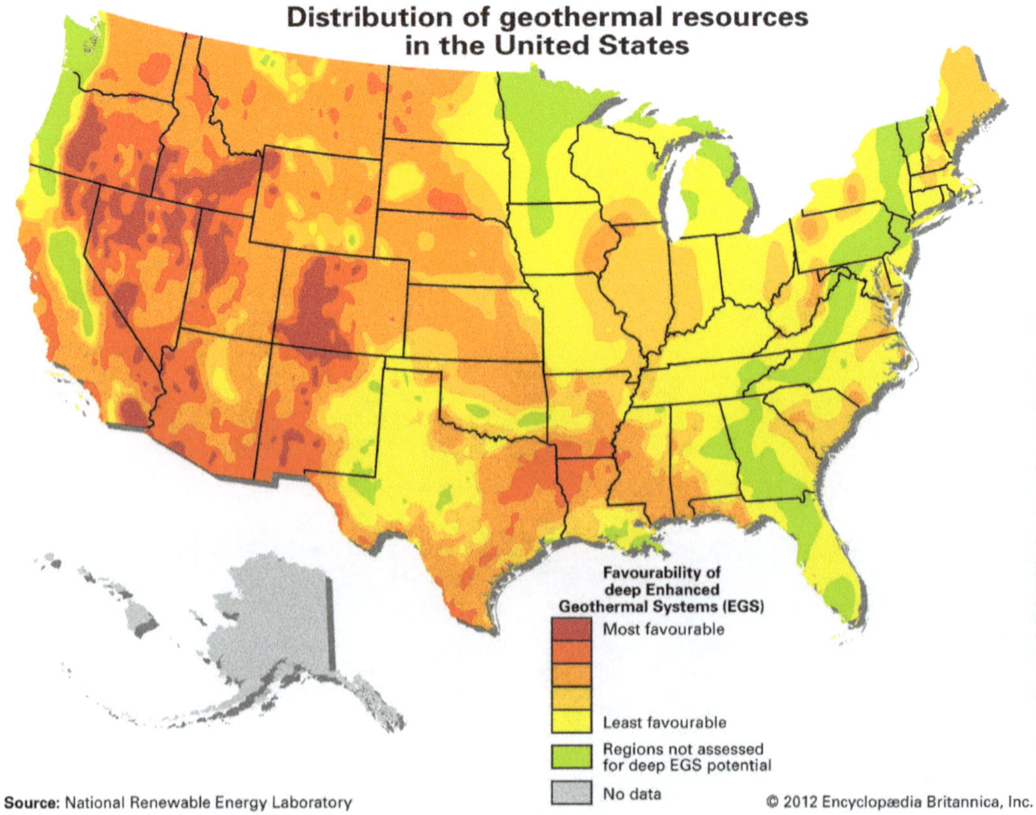

This map shows geothermal energy resources in the United States. As you can see, some areas have far more geothermal resources than others do.

crust (hot spots) such as Yellowstone National Park and the Hawaiian Islands. Areas near volcanic activity often have features that bring heat from deep inside Earth right to the surface, such as lava flows, geysers, or hot springs. In other places, the extraction of geothermal energy can be more challenging. For successful extraction, geothermal reservoirs must have adequate permeability or faults that allow fluids to rise close to the surface and an impermeable caprock to prevent the escape of heat. In addition, such reservoirs must be economically accessible (that is, within the range of drills).

The annual heat flow to the surface averages between 50 and 70 milliwatts (mW) per square meter worldwide. In contrast, incoming solar radiation striking Earth's surface provides 342 watts per square meter annually. The estimated amount of geothermal energy that can be recovered and utilized on the surface is roughly three times the world's annual consumption of all types of energy.

Geothermal energy is an alternative energy source. That means that it is one of several renewable power sources that can be used in place of fossil fuels and other traditional sources of energy, which are limited in supply and produce pollution and other environmental problems. Other alternative energy sources include solar power, wind power, and waterpower.

CHAPTER ONE

HEAT FROM INSIDE EARTH

Heat from Earth's interior is produced mainly by the radioactive decay of elements in Earth's crust and mantle and also by friction generated along the margins of continental plates. It generates surface phenomena such as lava flows, geysers, fumaroles, hot springs, and mud pots.

INSIDE EARTH

Earth is made up of three layers: the core, mantle, and crust. Temperatures and pressures rise with increasing depth inside the planet. At roughly 50 miles (80 kilometers) below the surface, the rock of the mantle is at about 2,500 degrees Fahrenheit (1,370 degrees Celsius) and becomes partly molten. Below about 150 to 200 miles (250–300 km), the mantle is under so much pressure that it becomes more rigid again.

Beneath the mantle, the material becomes much denser and liquefies. Scientists believe that this layer, called the outer core, consists of up to 90 percent molten iron and nickel, with some other elements such as sulfur mixed in. Finally, below about 3,200 miles (5,100 km) is the inner core. This hottest layer is estimated to be between 8,000°F and 12,000°F (about 4,400°C–6,600°C).

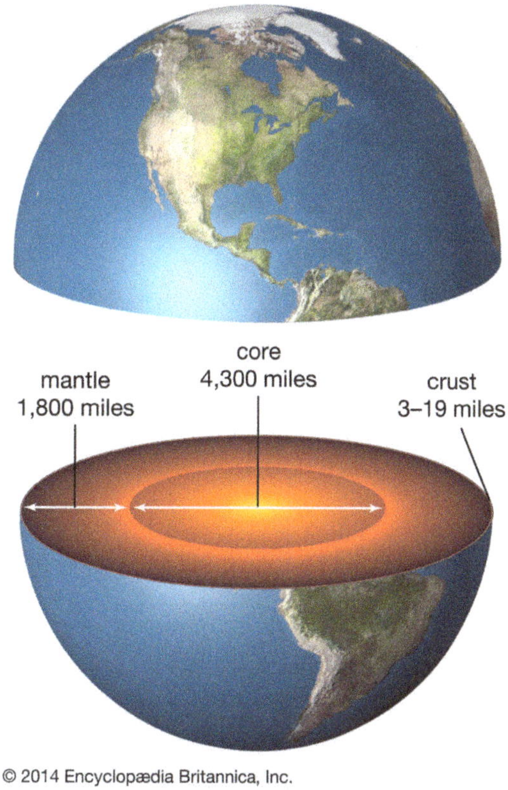

Earth's interior has three main layers: a relatively thin, rocky crust; a thick mantle; and a largely molten core. The measurements provided are averages.

Some of the heat in Earth's interior is left over from the planet's formation, and some is released from the outer core as iron and nickel slowly solidifies. Most of the heat, though, is believed to result from the decay of long-lived radioactive elements such as potassium, thorium, and uranium.

RADIOACTIVITY

Radioactivity is a feature of certain types of matter. All matter is made of chemical elements, and elements are made of atoms. Most atoms are stable. That is, they do not change over time. Radioactive atoms, however, change over time. Tiny subatomic particles and energy fly out of them naturally. The particles and energy that are released are a form of radiation.

The atoms are changed a little bit each time they release something. They keep giving off particles and energy until they are changed into a stable form. That process is called decay. The amount of time that each type of atom takes to decay varies greatly. It can be less than a second or millions of years. The measure of that rate is called a half-life. This refers to the time required for one half of a group of atoms to decay into a stable form.

Astronomers believe that these radioactive elements were formed in supernovas—catastrophic explosions of giant stars—that occurred before the solar system was formed. The uranium and other elements mixed with the clouds of gas and dust that ultimately collected together to form Earth.

PLATE TECTONICS

The crust and outermost mantle together are called the lithosphere, from the Greek word *lithos*, meaning "rock." The lithosphere is broken into rigid blocks, or plates, that essentially float on the denser material underneath and drift up against, alongside, over, or underneath other plates. The plates (and the

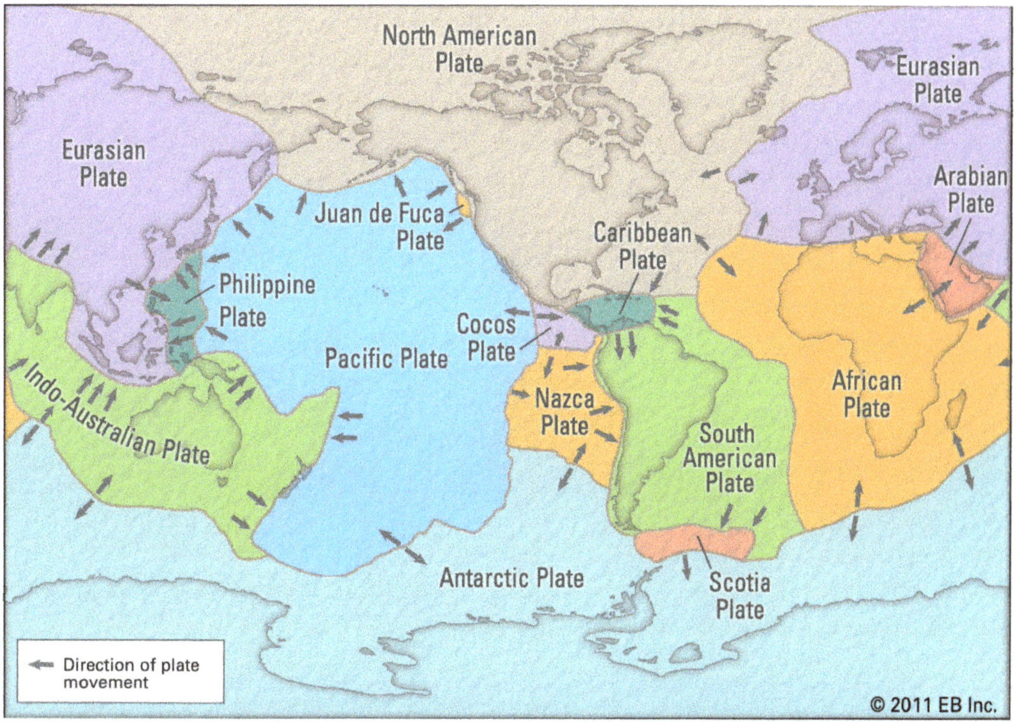

This map shows the tectonic plates that make up Earth's lithosphere. Earthquakes and volcanoes often happen along plate boundaries.

continents that rest on top of them) move at a rate of several inches per year. This process is known as plate tectonics.

The causes of plate motions are not completely understood, but a major factor appears to be giant convection cells (churning motions) in the mantle. Currents of hot material rise while currents of colder material sink, forming roughly circular cells—a common pattern of heat circulation that can also be seen in a pot of boiling water. In this way, the planet's interior redistributes heat resulting from the decay of radioactive elements.

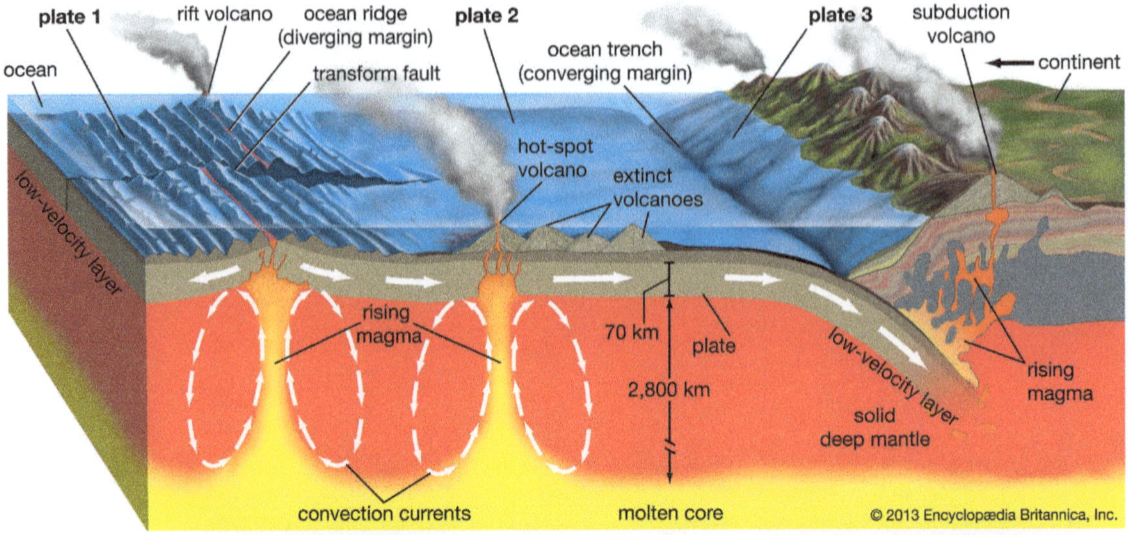

This diagram shows the relationship between volcanic activity and Earth's tectonic plates. As you can see, there are several ways in which molten rock and heat from deep inside Earth are brought to the surface.

VOLCANIC ACTIVITY

Molten rock located deep below the Earth's surface is called magma. It is formed when temperatures within Earth's crust or mantle are very hot and when pressure in places within those layers decreases. When a volcano erupts or a deep crack occurs in the Earth, magma rises and overflows. When it flows out of the volcano or crack, usually mixed with steam and gas, it is called lava.

Geophysical research suggests that volcanic magma forms near the base of Earth's crust and moves upward to a reservoir called a magma chamber before erupting at the surface. Magma rises because it is less dense than the rocks at lower depths, and its heat probably weakens surrounding rocks. The upward movement of magma may also be due to expanding gases within the molten rock or to chemical reactions that dissolve rocks above the magma. Volcanic material moves toward the surface through channelways and is extruded through vents at the surface.

HOT SPRINGS AND GEYSERS

In the late stages of volcanic activity, magma can heat circulating groundwater, producing hot springs

FUMAROLES

Fumaroles are closely related to hot springs and geysers. A fumarole is a vent in the Earth's surface from which steam and volcanic gases are released. Fumaroles are often found on active volcanoes, especially during periods of relative quiet between eruptions.

The water vapor that is ejected by fumaroles is usually groundwater. The groundwater gets heated by bodies of magma lying relatively close to the surface. The gases—carbon dioxide, sulfur dioxide, and hydrogen sulfide—are usually emitted directly from the magma. Sometimes a combination of these gases can be poisonous to plants and animals, but otherwise fumaroles are not dangerous.

and geysers. A hot spring, or thermal spring, is a spring that issues water at temperatures substantially higher than the air temperature of the surrounding region. Most hot springs discharge groundwater that is heated by shallow intrusions of magma in volcanic areas. Some thermal springs, however, are not related to volcanic activity. In such cases, deep circulation of water is thought to carry the water to the lower parts of the Earth's crust, where the temperature of the

This hot spring is on New Zealand's North Island. A wide belt of hot springs and geysers extends northeastward from the central volcanoes of the North Island to the sea.

rocks is high. A hot spring that spouts intermittent jets of water and steam with great force is known as a geyser.

Geysers are known for their often spectacular eruptions that throw water and steam high into the air. Old Faithful in Yellowstone National Park, the most famous geyser in the United States, erupts at intervals of 30 to 120 minutes. Each eruption lasts from 1.5 to 5.5 minutes. With each eruption it is estimated

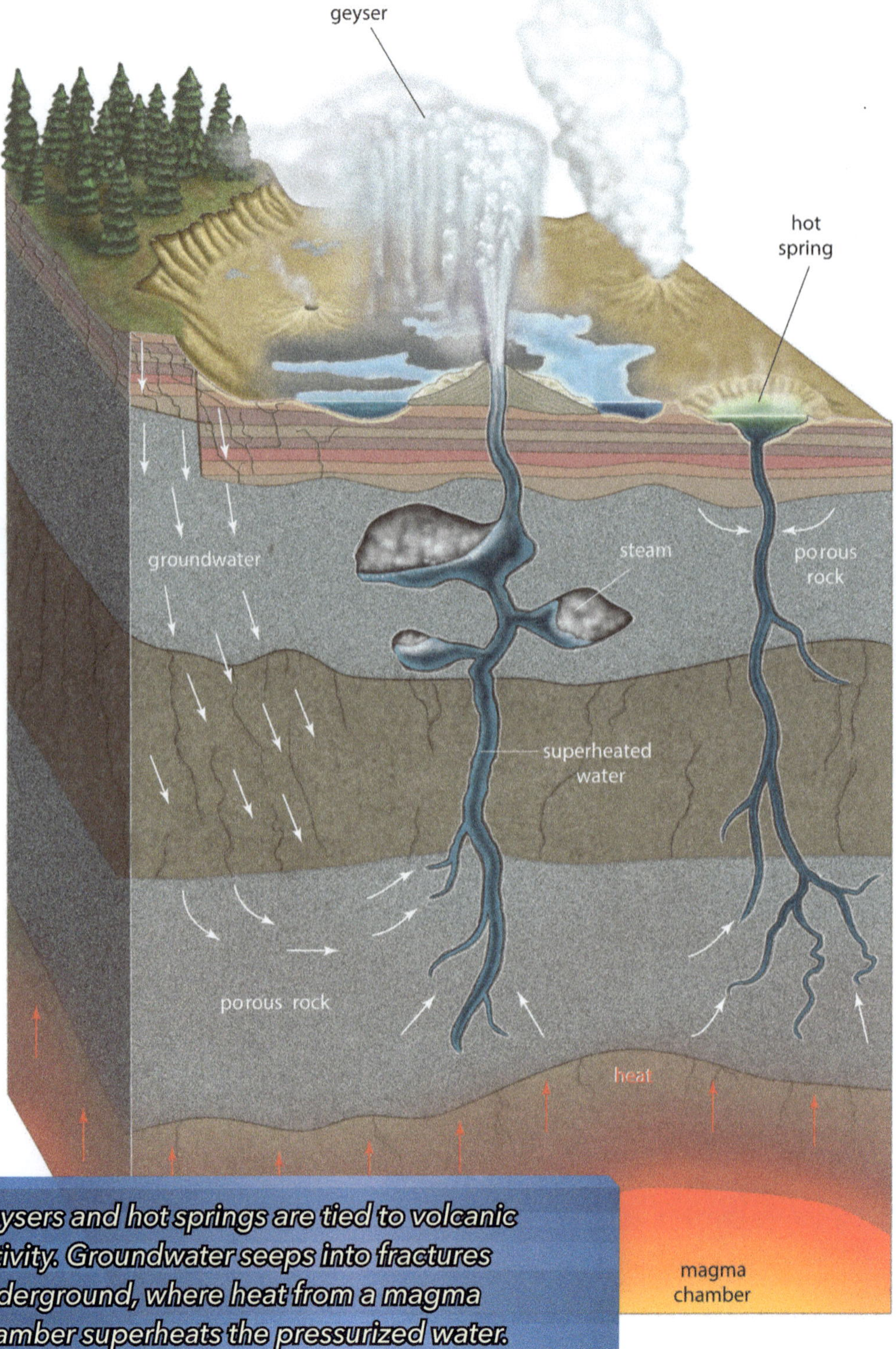

Geysers and hot springs are tied to volcanic activity. Groundwater seeps into fractures underground, where heat from a magma chamber superheats the pressurized water.

that about 3,700 to 8,400 gallons (14,000–32,000 liters) of water are discharged, with the fountainlike columns reaching heights averaging about 130–140 feet (40–43 meters), although eruption height can exceed 180 feet (55 m).

No two geysers behave in exactly the same way, and it is very difficult to study the system of underground passages that supplies any one of them. It is believed, however, that the underground structure of a geyser consists of a crooked tubelike opening that leads from the interior to the ground surface. Several small caverns or chambers may be connected to the tube. Groundwater partially fills the tube and some of the connecting caverns. The heated water is trapped under pressure in the crooked tube. Continued heating produces a water temperature above the boiling point, and the steam so produced develops enough pressure to eject a small amount of water to the surface. This expulsion of water in the initial upsurge reduces pressure on the superheated water in the tube. The reduction in pressure causes the remaining water to boil explosively to the point where it drives a column of water and steam, called the geyser jet, into the air. The eruption continues until water and steam are driven out of the tube and storage caverns.

CHAPTER TWO

GEOTHERMAL ENERGY USE

Geothermal energy use can be divided into three categories: direct-use applications, geothermal heat pumps (GHPs), and electric power generation.

DIRECT USE

Probably the most widely used set of applications involves the direct use of heated water from the ground without the need for any specialized equipment. All direct-use applications make use of low-temperature geothermal resources, which range between about 122°F and 302°F (50°C –150°C). Such low-temperature geothermal water and steam have been used to warm single buildings, as well as whole districts where numerous buildings are heated from

These public pools in Beitou, Taiwan, are fed by hot springs. Beitou is near Taiwan's capital city, Taipei. Its hot springs have made it a popular recreation area.

a central supply source. In addition, many swimming pools, therapeutic facilities at spas, greenhouses, and aquaculture ponds around the world have been heated with geothermal resources. Other direct uses of geothermal energy include cooking, industrial applications (such as drying fruit, vegetables, and timber), milk pasteurization, and large-scale snow melting. For many of those activities, hot water is often used directly in the heating system, or it may be used in conjunction with a heat exchanger, which transfers heat when there are problematic minerals and gases such as hydrogen sulfide mixed in with the fluid.

GEOTHERMAL HEAT PUMPS

GHPs take advantage of the relatively stable moderate temperature conditions that occur within the first 1,000 feet (300 m) of the surface to heat buildings in the winter and cool them in the summer. In that part of the lithosphere, rocks and groundwater occur at temperatures between 41°F and 86°F (5°C–30°C). At shallower depths where most GHPs are found, such as within 20 feet (6 m) of Earth's surface, the ground maintains a near-constant temperature of 50°F to 60°F (10°C–16°C). Consequently, that heat can be used to help warm buildings during the colder months of the year when the air temperature falls below that of the ground. Similarly, during the warmer months of the year, warm air can be drawn from a building and circulated underground, where it loses much of its heat and is returned.

A GHP system is made up of a heat exchanger (a loop of pipes buried in the ground) and a pump. The heat exchanger transfers heat energy between

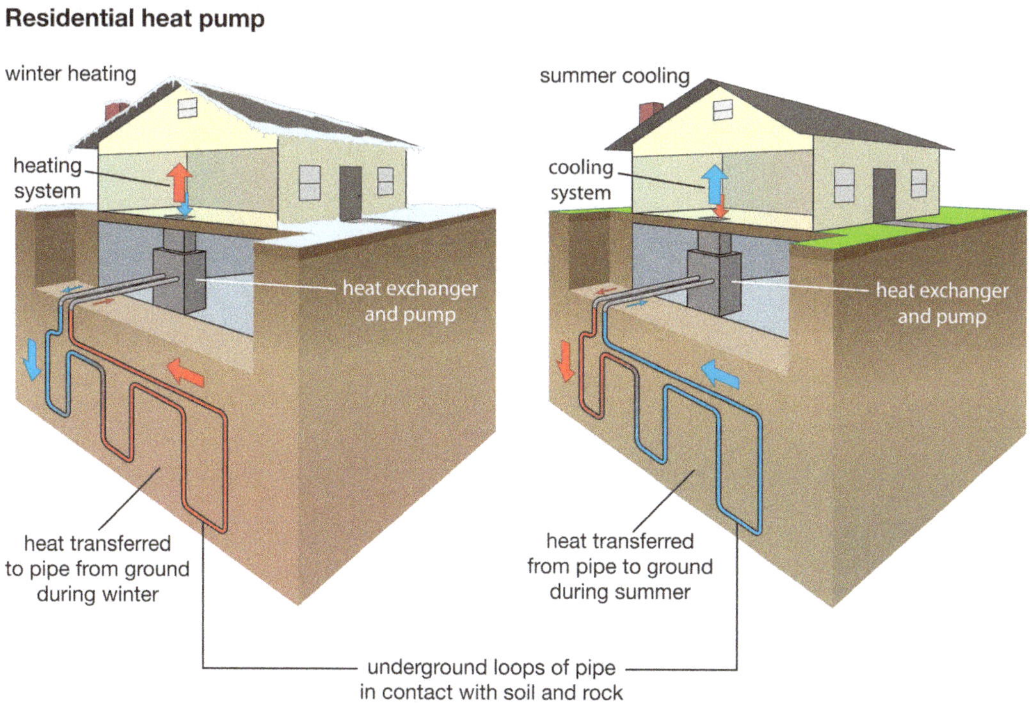

This diagram shows how a geothermal heat pump system can be used for both summer cooling and winter heating.

the ground and air at the surface by means of a fluid that circulates through the pipes. The fluid used is often water or a combination of water and antifreeze. During warmer months, heat from warm air is transferred to the heat exchanger and into the fluid. As it moves through the pipes, the heat is dispersed to the rocks, soil, and groundwater. The

EXTRACTION

The heated fluid from a geothermal resource is tapped by drilling wells, sometimes as deep as 30,000 feet (9,100 m), and is extracted by pumping or by natural artesian flow (where the weight of the water forces it to the surface). Water and steam are then piped to the power plant to generate electricity or through insulated pipelines—which may be buried or placed aboveground—for use in heating and cooling applications.

In general, electric power plant pipelines are limited to roughly 1 mile (1.6 km) in length to minimize heat loss in the steam. However, direct-use pipelines spanning several miles (km) have been installed with a temperature loss of less than 3.6°F–9°F (-15.8°C–-12.8°C), depending on the flow rate.

The most economically efficient facilities are located close to the geothermal resource to minimize the expense of constructing long pipelines. In the case of electric power generation, costs can be kept down by locating the facility near electrical transmission lines to transmit the electricity to market.

pump is reversed during the colder months. Heat energy stored in the relatively warm ground raises the temperature of the fluid. The fluid then transfers this energy to the heat pump, which warms the air inside the building.

GHPs have several advantages over more conventional heating and air-conditioning systems. They are very efficient, using 25–50 percent less electricity than comparable conventional heating and cooling systems, and they produce less pollution. According to the U.S. Environmental Protection Agency in 2010, the reduction in energy use associated with GHPs translated into as much as a 44 percent decrease in greenhouse gas emissions compared with air-source heat pumps (which transfer heat between indoor and outdoor air). In addition, when compared with electric resistance heating systems (which convert electricity to heat) coupled with standard air-conditioning systems, GHPs produce up to 72 percent fewer greenhouse gas emissions.

ELECTRIC POWER GENERATION

Depending upon the temperature and the fluid (steam) flow, geothermal energy can be used to

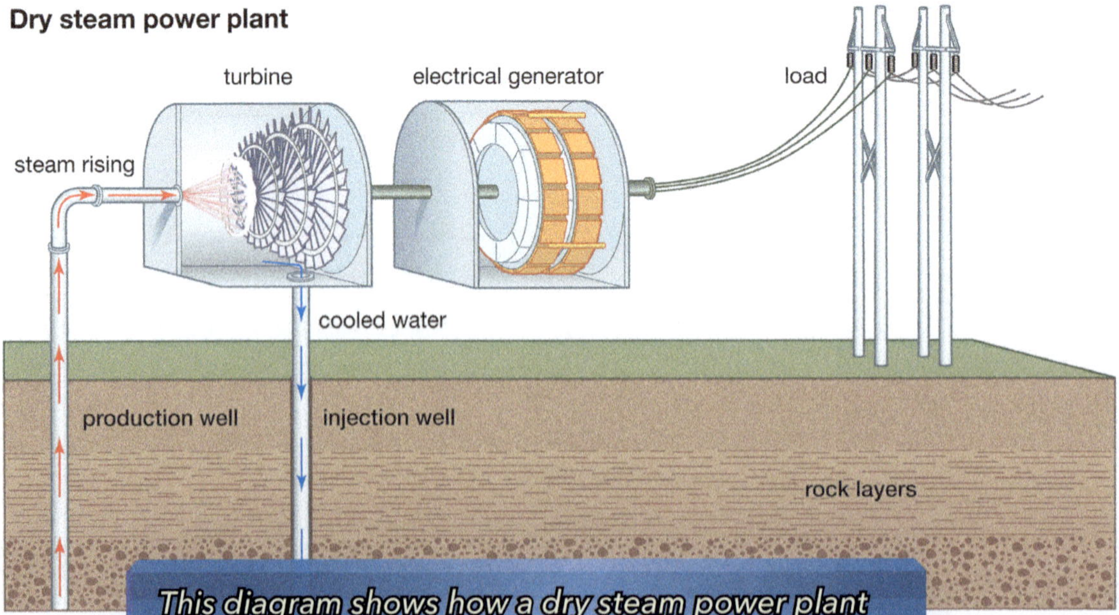

This diagram shows how a dry steam power plant works. Dry steam power plants are the oldest type of geothermal power plants.

generate electricity. Geothermal power plants can produce electricity in three ways. Despite their differences in design, all three control the behavior of steam and use it to drive electrical generators, and the excess water vapor at the end of each process is condensed and returned to the ground, where it is reheated for later use.

Some geothermal power plants simply collect rising steam from the ground. In such "dry steam" operations, the heated water vapor is funneled directly into a turbine that drives an electrical gen-

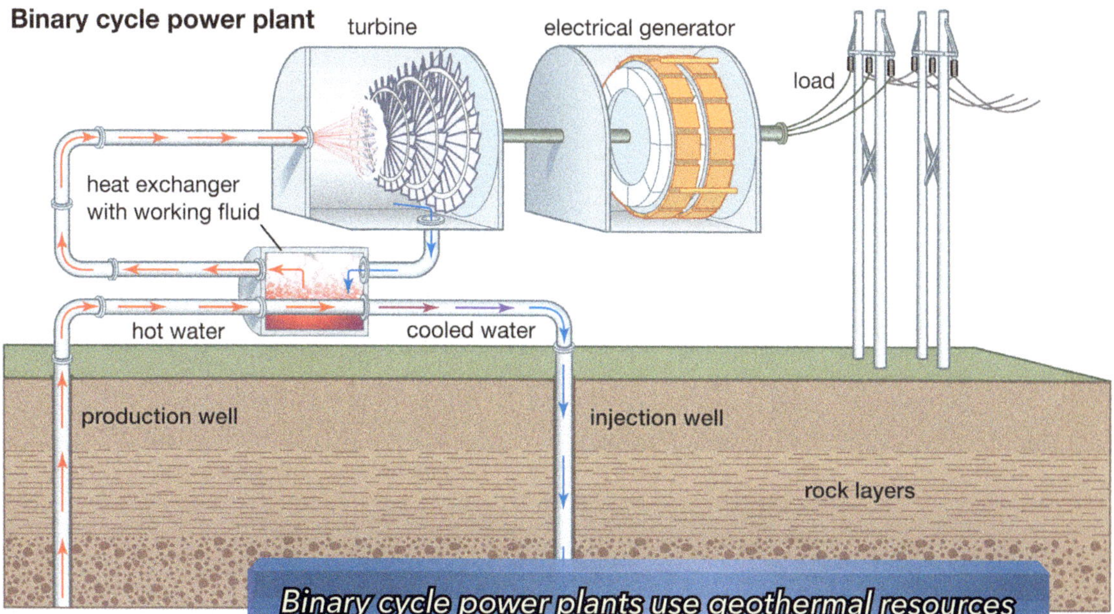

Binary cycle power plants use geothermal resources to heat a secondary fluid. They are the type of geothermal plant most often built today.

erator. Other power plants, built around the flash steam and binary cycle designs, use a mixture of steam and heated water ("wet steam") extracted from the ground to start the electrical generation process.

In flash steam power plants, pressurized high-temperature water is drawn from beneath the surface into containers at the surface, called flash tanks, where the sudden decrease in pressure causes the liquid water to "flash," or vaporize, into steam. The steam is then used to power the turbine-generator set.

In contrast, binary-cycle power plants use steam driven off a secondary working fluid (such as ammonia and hydrocarbons) contained within a closed loop of pipes to power the turbine-generator set. In this process, geothermally heated water is drawn up through a different set of pipes, and much of the energy stored in the heated water is transferred to the working fluid through a heat exchanger. The working fluid then vaporizes. After the vapor from the working fluid passes through the turbine, it is recondensed and piped back to the heat exchanger.

Electrical power usually requires water heated above 347°F (175°C) to be economical. In geothermal plants using the Organic Rankine Cycle (ORC), a special type of binary-cycle technology that utilizes lower-temperature heat sources (such as biomass combustion and industrial waste heat), water temperatures as low as 185°F–194°F (85°C–90°C) may be used.

CHAPTER THREE

THE HISTORY OF GEOTHERMAL ENERGY

Geothermal energy from natural pools and hot springs has long been used for cooking, bathing, and warmth. There is evidence that Native Americans used geothermal energy for cooking as early as 10,000 years ago. In ancient times, the Greeks and Romans used baths heated by hot springs. Examples of geothermal space heating date at least as far back as the Roman city of Pompeii during the first century CE. Such uses of geothermal energy were initially limited to sites where hot water and steam were accessible.

SPAS

A spa is a spring or resort with thermal or mineral water used for drinking and bathing. Springs have

These people are relaxing in a geothermal pool at the Blue Lagoon resort, in Iceland. Iceland has more hot springs than any other country.

been considered places of healing at many times and in all parts of the world. Japan has several thousand hot springs, many of which have been converted into spas or public baths. In the West, the practice of "taking the waters" for therapeutic purposes reached its heyday in the nineteenth century. The spas of Europe and the United States with the greatest popularity were those with thermal springs.

HOT SPRINGS NATIONAL PARK

The springs at Hot Springs National Park in central Arkansas, long used by the Indians and probably visited by Hernando de Soto in 1541, drew Spanish and French visitors in search of health benefits in the eighteenth century. The area was mapped in 1804 by an expedition led by the Americans William Dunbar and George Hunter. Permanent settlement of the site dates from 1807.

GEOTHERMAL HEAT

Although the world's first district heating system was installed at Chaudes-Aigues, France, in the fourteenth century, it was not until the late nineteenth century that other cities, as well as industries, began to realize the economic potential of geothermal resources. Geothermal heat was delivered to the first residences in the United States in 1892, to Warm Springs Avenue in Boise, Idaho, and most of the city used geothermal heat by 1970. The largest and most-famous geothermal district heating system is

Strikingly modern and clean in appearance, the city of Reykjavík is largely built of concrete and is heated by hot water piped from nearby hot springs.

in Reykjavík, Iceland, where 99 percent of the city received geothermal water for space heating starting in the 1930s. Early industrial direct-use applications include the extraction of borate compounds from geothermal fluids at Larderello, Italy, during the early nineteenth century.

By 2014 more than 80 countries used geothermal energy either directly or in conjunction with GHPs, the leaders being the United States, China,

Sweden, Japan, Turkey, and Iceland. The total worldwide installed capacity for direct use in 2010 was about 50,000 megawatts thermal (MWt) utilizing about 120,000 gigawatt-hours per year (432,000 terajoules per year), producing an annual utilization factor—the annual energy produced by the plant (in megawatt-hours) divided by the installed capacity of the plant (in megawatts [MW]) multiplied by 8,760 hours—of 28 percent in the heating mode.

GENERATING ELECTRICITY

The first geothermal electric power generation was in Larderello, Italy, with the development of an experimental plant in 1904; the first commercial use of that technology occurred there in 1913 with the construction of a plant that produced 250 kilowatts (kW). Geothermal power plants were commissioned in New Zealand starting in 1958 and at The Geysers in northern California in 1960. The Italian and American plants were dry steam facilities, where low-permeability reservoirs produced only steam. In New Zealand, however, high-temperature and high-pressure water emerges naturally as a mixture made up of 80 percent superheated water and 20 percent steam. The steam coming directly from the ground is used for

The Wairakei geothermal electric power generating station is located in the Taupo Volcanic Zone, a highly volcanic area on New Zealand's North Island.

power generation right away. It is sent to the power plant through pipes. In contrast, the superheated water from the ground is separated from the mixture and flashed into steam. Most geothermal plants at present are of this latter "wet steam" type.

By the early twenty-first century, geothermal energy was used to produce electricity in 24 countries, the leaders being the United States, the Philippines, Indonesia, Mexico, Italy, and New Zealand. The total worldwide installed capacity in 2010 for electrical power generation was about 11,000 MW, producing about 68,000 gigawatt-hours per year for a utilization factor of 71 percent (i.e., equivalent to 6,220 full-load operating hours annually). Many geothermal fields have utilization factors around 95 percent (equivalent to 8,322 full-load operating hours annually), the highest for any form of renewable energy. The "waste" fluid from the power plant is often used for lower-temperature applications, such as the bottom cycle in a binary-cycle plant, before being injected back into the reservoir. Such cascaded uses can be found in the United States, Iceland, and Germany.

CHAPTER FOUR

THE FUTURE OF GEOTHERMAL ENERGY

Geothermal energy is one of several alternative energy sources that people are using instead of fossil fuels. However, like all energy sources, geothermal energy is not without its drawbacks. While Earth contains tremendous amounts of heat energy, only a tiny portion of it is near enough to the surface to be easily exploited—and that which is exploitable is found in a relatively small number of specific locations.

WHY WE NEED ALTERNATIVE ENERGY

Growing concern over the world's ever-increasing energy needs and the prospect of rapidly dwindling reserves of oil, natural gas, and uranium fuel have prompted efforts to develop viable alternative energy sources, including geothermal energy. The volatility and uncertainty of the petroleum fuel supply were dramatically brought to the fore during the energy crisis of the 1970s caused by the abrupt curtailment of oil shipments from the Middle East to many of the highly industrialized nations of the world.

The use of fossil fuels, such as the gasoline in cars and trucks, produces both pollution and the greenhouse gases that cause global warming.

It also has been recognized that the heavy reliance on fossil fuels has had an adverse impact on the environment. Gasoline engines and steam-turbine power plants that burn coal or natural gas emit substantial amounts of sulfur dioxide and nitrogen oxides into the atmosphere. When these gases combine with atmospheric water vapor, they form sulfuric acid and nitric acids, giving rise to highly acidic precipitation. The combustion of fossil fuels also releases carbon dioxide. The amount of this gas in the atmosphere has steadily risen since the mid-1800s largely as a result of the growing consumption of coal, oil, and natural gas. The atmospheric buildup of carbon dioxide (along with other industrial gases) induces a greenhouse effect, raising the surface temperature of the Earth by increasing the amount of heat trapped in the lower atmosphere. This condition could bring about climatic changes with serious repercussions for natural and agricultural ecosystems.

ENVIRONMENTAL EFFECTS AND ECONOMIC COSTS

The environmental effects of geothermal development and power generation include the changes in land use associated with exploration and plant construction, noise and sight pollution, the discharge of water and gases, the production of foul odors, and soil subsidence. Most of those effects, however, can be mitigated with current technology so that geothermal uses have no more than a minimal impact on the environment. For example, Klamath Falls, Oregon, has

GEOTHERMAL HEAT PUMPS AND THE ENVIRONMENT

GHPs have a very minimal effect on the environment, because they make use of shallow geothermal resources within about 330 feet (100 m) of the surface. GHPs cause only small temperature changes to the groundwater or rocks and soil in the ground. In closed-loop systems the ground temperature around the vertical boreholes is slightly increased or decreased. The direction of the temperature change is governed by whether the system is dominated by heating (which would be the case in colder regions) or cooling (which would be the case in warmer regions). With balanced heating and cooling loads, the ground temperatures will remain stable. Likewise, open-loop systems using groundwater or lake water would have very little effect on temperature, especially in regions characterized by high groundwater flows.

approximately 600 geothermal wells for residential space heating. The city has also invested in a district heating system and a downtown snow-melting system, and it provides heating to local businesses. However, none of the systems used to supply and deliver

The sidewalks leading up to the county administrative building in Klamath Falls are kept clear of snow thanks to the geothermal heating system running under them.

geothermal energy are visible in town.

Comparing the benefits of geothermal energy with other renewable energy sources, the main advantage of geothermal energy is that its base load is available 24 hours per day, 7 days per week, whereas solar and wind are available only about one-third of the time. In addition, the cost of geothermal energy varies between 5 and 10 cents per kilowatt-hour, which can be competitive with other energy sources, such as coal. The main disadvantage of geothermal energy development is the high initial investment cost in constructing the facilities and infrastructure and the high risk of proving the resources. (Geothermal resources in low-permeability rocks are often found, and exploration activities often drill "dry" holes—that is, holes that produce steam in amounts too low to be exploited economically.) However, once the resource is proven, the annual cost of fuel (that is, hot water and steam) is low and tends not to escalate in price.

The Mutnovskaya Geothermal Power Station is in Russia's Kamchatka region. The area has a lot of geothermal activity, including active volcanoes, hot springs, and geysers.

THE CHALLENGE OF SUSTAINABILITY

The amount of usable energy from geothermal sources varies with depth and by extraction method. The increase in temperature of rocks and other materials underground averages 58°F–86°F per mile (14°C–30°C/km) depth worldwide in the upper part of the lithosphere, and this rate of increase is much higher in most of Earth's known geothermal areas. Normally, heat extraction requires a fluid (or steam) to

The geothermal power plant in Larderello, Italy, was built more than a century ago, but continues to supply power today.

bring the energy to the surface. Locating and developing geothermal resources can be challenging. This is especially true for the high-temperature resources needed for generating electricity. Such resources are typically limited to parts of the world characterized by recent volcanic activity or located along plate boundaries or within crustal hot spots. Even though there is a continuous source of heat within Earth, the extraction rate of the heated fluids and steam can exceed the replenishment rate, and, thus, use of the resource must be managed sustainably.

Normally, geothermal resources can be used for 20 to 30 years. However, the energy output may decrease with time, making continued development uneconomical. On the other hand, geothermal electric power has been produced continually from the Larderello geothermal field since the early 1900s and at The Geysers since 1960. Although there has been a decline in both of those fields, this problem has been partially overcome by drilling new wells and by recharging the water supply. At The Geysers, electrical capacity declined from 1,800 MW to approximately 1,000 MW, but about 200 MW of capacity was returned by placing the field under one operator and constructing pipelines to deliver wastewater for recharging the reservoir. Projects such as the Reykjavík district heating system have been operating since the 1930s with little change in the output, and the Oregon Institute of Technology geothermal heating system has been operating since the 1950s with no change in production. Thus, with proper management, geothermal resources can be sustainable for many years, and they can even recover if use is suspended for a period of time.

GLOSSARY

AQUACULTURE The cultivation of living things (as fish or shellfish) naturally occurring in water.

ATOM One of the tiny particles that are the basic building blocks of all matter. Atoms can be combined with other atoms to form molecules, but they cannot be divided into smaller parts by ordinary means.

BIOMASS Plant materials and animal waste that can be used as source of fuel.

CAPROCK An overlying rock layer that is usually hard to penetrate.

CHEMICAL REACTION A process in which one or more substances are converted to one or more different substances.

COMBUSTION A chemical reaction that produces heat and light, such as fire.

CONDENSE To change from a gas to a liquid.

FLUID A substance tending to flow or take the shape of its container. Liquids and gases are fluids.

FRICTION The force that resists motion between bodies in contact.

GENERATOR A machine by which mechanical energy is changed into electrical energy.

GRADIENT A continuous graded change in measure, activity, or substance.

GREENHOUSE EFFECT The warming of Earth's surface and the air above it, caused by gases in the air that trap energy from the sun.

GROUNDWATER Water within the earth that supplies wells and springs.

HYDROCARBON An organic compound containing only carbon and hydrogen.

INFRASTRUCTURE The system of public works of a country, state, or region.

INTRUSION The entry by force of melted rock into or between other rock formations.

MOLTEN Melted, especially by very great heat.

PERMEABILITY Permitting liquids or gases to pass through pores or openings.

RADIATION The process of giving off radiant energy in the form of waves or particles.

RESERVOIR A place where something collects or is kept in store.

SUBATOMIC PARTICLES Tiny particles that make up atoms, such as protons, electrons, and neutrons.

SUPERHEAT To heat (steam) to a higher temperature than the normal boiling point of water.

THERAPEUTIC Relating to the treatment of diseases or disorders by using healing agents or methods.

TURBINE An engine whose central driving shaft is fitted with a series of blades spun around by the pressure of a fluid (as water, steam, or air).

FOR MORE INFORMATION

Bard, Mariel. *Geothermal Energy: Harnessing the Power of Earth's Heat* (Powered Up! A STEM Approach to Energy Sources). New York, NY: PowerKids Press, 2018.

Bow, James. *Energy from Earth's Core: Geothermal Energy* (Next Generation Energy). New York, NY: Crabtree Publishing Company, 2016.

Brundle, Harriet. *Renewable Energy*. New York, NY: KidHaven Publishing, 2018.

Centore, Michael. *Renewable Energy* (North American Natural Resources). Broomall, PA: Mason Crest, 2016.

Dickmann, Nancy. *Harnessing Geothermal Energy* (Future of Power). New York, NY: PowerKids Press, 2017.

Doeden, Matt. *Finding Out About Geothermal Energy* (Searchlight Books: What Are Energy Sources?). Minneapolis, MN: Lerner Publications Company, 2015.

Grady, Colin. *Geothermal Power* (Saving the Planet through Green Energy). New York, NY: Enslow Publishing, 2017.

Howell, Izzi. *Volcano Geo Facts* (Geofacts) New York, NY: Crabtree Publishing Company, 2018.

Jackson, Tom. *The Basics of Atoms and Molecules* (Core Concepts). New York, NY: Rosen Publishing, 2014.

Mangor, Jodie. *Geothermal Energy* (Core Library: Alternative Energy) Minneapolis, MN: ABDO Publishing, 2017.

Mason, Helen. *Energy Entrepreneurs* (Science and Technology Start-Up Stars). New York, NY: Crabtree Publishing Company, 2018.

Otfinoski, Steven. *Wind, Solar, and Geothermal Power: From Concept to Consumer.* New York, NY: Children's Press, 2016.

Oxlade, Chris. *Volcanoes* (100 Facts You Should Know). New York, NY: Gareth Stevens Publishing, 2015.

Reilly, Kathleen M. *Fault Lines & Tectonic Plates: Discover What Happens When the Earth's Crust Moves, With 25 Projects* (Build It Yourself). White River Junction, VT: Nomad Press, 2017.

Sawyer, Ava. *Human Environmental Impact: How We Affect Earth* (Fact Finders: Humans and Our Planet). North Mankato, MN: Capstone Press, 2018.

Shea, Therese. *Geysers and Hot Springs* (Nature's Mysteries). New York, NY: Britannica Educational Publishing, 2017.

WEBSITES

Geothermal Energy Association
http://www.geo-energy.org/
Facebook: @geothermalenergyassociation;
Twitter: @geoenergist

International Energy Agency
https://www.iea.org/topics/renewables/subtopics/geothermal/
Facebook: @internationalenergyagency; Twitter: @IEA

U.S. Department of Energy
https://www.energy.gov/science-innovation/energy-sources/renewable-energy/geothermal
Facebook: @energygov; Instagram, Twitter: @energy

U.S. Energy Information Administration
https://www.eia.gov/energyexplained/index-cfm?page=geothermal_home
Facebook, Twitter: @eeiagov

INDEX